Original Title: Footsteps in the Sand

Copyright © 2024 Book Fairy Publishing
All rights reserved.

Editors: Theodor Taimla
Autor: Rachelle Randvee
ISBN 978-9916-748-80-0

Footsteps in the Sand

Rachelle Randvee

Seaside Echoes

Waves lap softly on the shore,
Whispered secrets, nothing more.
Sunset paints a golden ray,
Kissing dreams that drift away.

Seagulls call with voices free,
Their songs echo o'er the sea.
Footprints trace a fleeting path,
Slowly washed away post-bath.

Shells lie scattered, stories told,
Of ancient tides and hearts so bold.
Mermaid tales and whispered winds,
Lovers' promises, it rescinds.

Glimpses in the Sandscape

Dunes ripple under pastel skies,
Where whispers of the ocean rise.
Grains of sand like stars arrayed,
In twilight's gentle, dim parade.

Moonlight dances on the crest,
Glimpses of a shore at rest.
Silent waves in dark embrace,
Weave a tapestry of grace.

Night reveals its hidden gems,
In the sand, the world condemns.
Footprints fade with morning's sigh,
Glimpses lost as dreams fly by.

Transient Treads

Along the edge where waters meet,
Transient treads of wandering feet.
Each step a mark, a moment brief,
Written in the sand, a leaf.

Ephemeral journeys, come and pass,
Patterns in the rippling glass.
Time it weaves, a shifting mate,
Footfalls swallowed by their fate.

Whispers of a distant chat,
Stories lie where footsteps sat.
Voyagers to the end unknown,
Transient treads of hearts alone.

Fragments of Footprints

On a shore where echoes blend,
Footprints weave, then tales amend.
Fragments left by passing souls,
Whispered dreams in secret shoals.

Patterns drawn by fleeting hands,
Shifting shapes in shifting sands.
Every step a trace of life,
Moments carved against the strife.

Sunrise brings its gentle hues,
Fragments woven in the news.
Footprints vanish, yet they stay,
In the heart, they find their way.

Whispers Beneath Waves

In shadows where the ocean sighs,
A whisper travels, deep and wise.
Beneath the waves, the ancient lore,
Resounds upon the sandy shore.

Moonbeams dance on crests of blue,
Lost in tides, both old and new.
Secrets kept in currents' sway,
Followed by the break of day.

Treasures lie in shells and sand,
Marking places where dreams stand.
In the silence, voices blend,
Where sea and sky forever mend.

Delicate Imprints

Upon the glass, a breath remains,
A mark that time cannot contain.
Fleeting whispers left in trace,
Moments etched in fragile grace.

Petals fall with soft descent,
Emblems of the transient.
Life's imprints, a tender touch,
Captured in a moment's clutch.

Footsteps fade on silken strands,
Waves dissolve what once did stand.
Yet in hearts, those marks we keep,
Forever cherished, ever deep.

Journeys in Each Grain

In every speck that gleams with gold,
Lies a journey yet untold.
Windswept paths across the dunes,
Where the desert hums its tunes.

Each grain whispers of a quest,
Adventures lodged within its crest.
Stories blend in arcs and swirls,
Bound within this world of pearls.

Through the sands, our spirits climb,
Tracing echoes, passing time.
In each grain, life's essence stays,
Guiding us through endless days.

Unseen Pathways

Through the woods, a silent call,
Guides us where the shadows fall.
Paths unseen by mortal sight,
Illuminated in the night.

Steps we take in moonlit glades,
Lead us through the secret shades.
Nature's whispers, pure and clear,
Show us that we need not fear.

In the spaces in-between,
Magic lies, serene, unseen.
Follow where the heart does stray,
Wander on, the unseen way.

Transient Ripples

In the mirror of twilight skies,
A ripple brews as daylight flies.
Whispers smooth the silent stream,
Dances part like a transient dream.

Ephemeral waves kiss the shore,
Carrying tales of evermore.
The silent moon looks down in grace,
Marking time in pale embrace.

Rocks are bathed in silver mist,
By ripples spawned from nature's twist.
Life unfurls in moments brief,
Transient joys, transient grief.

Stories in the Sand

Wind carries whispers near and far,
Sands shift with tales bizarre.
Each grain holds secrets strange,
Crafted by time's endless range.

Footprints etch a timeless scroll,
Where heartbeats play their role.
Moments held by grains so small,
Binding stories, one and all.

Waves sweep clean the ancient slate,
Yet new stories resonate.
In sands of time, all tales blend,
Circling beginnings without end.

Etched by the Sea

Eternal rhythms etch the shore,
Lines of stories, then and more.
In the foam's embrace of sand,
Dreams and sorrows hand in hand.

Oblivion's sketch along the bay,
Resembles lives once found stray.
Each wave inscribes a fleeting verse,
Lost again in nature's terse.

Patterns fade, and then renew,
Under skies of cerulean blue.
Sea's endless pen, without cease,
Writes of chaos, shapes of peace.

Swept Away Traces

Gone are traces left behind,
Swept away by ocean's mind.
Silent tides possess the art,
Brushing with a gentle heart.

Ephemeral marks of joy and pain,
Carried to the sea's domain.
None can keep the fleeting day,
For time and tide will always sway.

Memory's beach, washed anew,
By the waves of azure hue.
Leaving silhouettes of grace,
Swept away without a trace.

Temporal Sand Chronicles

Grains of time slip through my hand
Moments lost in golden sand
Echoes of a distant past
Fleeting shadows never last

Life like tides will ebb and flow
Catching whispers as they go
In the hourglass we stand
Ever counting grains of sand

Memory's a fragile thread
Connecting whispers of the dead
As the future winds do call
Time will conquer, standing tall

Dancing on the Shoreline

Waves caress the sleepy land
Footsteps vanish in the sand
Moonlight waltz on ocean crest
Nature's heartbeat never rests

Seagulls serenade the dawn
While the night is gently drawn
Radiant stars fade away
Heralding a brand new day

Children play in the twilight
Chasing dreams that take to flight
Dancing where the seas do meet
Waves and laughter at our feet

Prints of the Past

Ancient echoes, whispers faint
Memories of a life now quaint
Carved in stone and weathered wood
Silent markers where they stood

Stories told by candlelight
In the stillness of the night
Keep the ghosts of yesteryear
Draped in shadows, crystal clear

Time erases, leaves a trace
Of the lives we can't replace
In the heart these prints will stay
Guiding us along the way

Momentary Paths

On the road to worlds unknown
Footsteps chart the ground we've sown
Transient paths of fleeting grace
Guiding us from place to place

Stars above our midnight guide
In their glow we gently glide
Journey's end forever near
Chasing dreams without a fear

Each new dawn a canvas bright
Painted roads in morning light
Momentary paths we tread
Whisper tales of where we've led

Silent Coastal Stroll

The moonlight guides my steps tonight,
A path of silver, soft and bright.
Waves whisper secrets to the shore,
Their ancient tales forevermore.

Cool breeze that carries ocean's scent,
With each breath, a moment spent.
Stars above in vast array,
Illuminate the water's sway.

Footprints left in shifting sand,
Ephemeral marks by nature's hand.
The vast expanse where sea meets sky,
An endless canvas to pass by.

Solitude, my faithful friend,
In this peace, no need to mend.
Silent whispers in the wind,
A coastal symphony, unique and pinned.

Impressions of the Coast

Golden sun dips into the waves,
Bathing shores in fleeting rays.
Seagulls cry their mournful tune,
Echoes fade beneath the moon.

Rocks weathered by time's gentle hand,
Stand steadfast defending the sand.
Foams embrace with passionate kiss,
Moments of fleeting ocean bliss.

Shells collect in tidal pools,
Nature's gems, what precious jewels.
Each one tells a silent tale,
Of whispered breezes and salt-sweet gale.

Palm trees sway in evening gust,
Bark encrusted with windblown dust.
Hearts that wander find their rest,
By the sea's unending quest.

Timeless Beach Paths

Sand beneath my feet so warm,
Where tides and winds perform.
Paths once trod by countless souls,
Their stories mingling with the shoals.

Sunset hues paint skies ablaze,
Mirrors on the water's glaze.
Each footprint marks a brief journey,
In a world of ebb and eternity.

Birds embark on wind's swift ride,
Guided by the ocean's tide.
Their calls dissolve in dusk's embrace,
As twilight shadows interlace.

Timeless paths where hearts convene,
On tranquil shores ever serene.
Infinity in grains of sand,
Held gently in nature's hand.

Shoreline Shadows

Shadows stretch across the sand,
Drawn by twilight's gentle hand.
Every wave a whispered dream,
In the fading daylight's beam.

Footsteps silent in their tread,
Following where shadows led.
The horizon's edge in glowing fire,
Speaks of an eternal desire.

Flickering stars watch over waves,
Guardians of hidden caves.
Tidal lullabies softly sing,
Of moonlight's lunar ring.

Whispers of a day now past,
In memory's embrace held fast.
Silent echoes, soft and low,
In shadows cast upon the shore.

Remembrance by the Sea

Waves whisper tales under moonlit glow
Soft sands carry footprints faint and slow
Seagulls cry as they soar high and free
Memories dance in the heart by the sea

Shells gleam with secrets of distant shores
Timeless echoes revive forgotten scores
Salt-kissed breezes weave through the air
In this place, we leave our burdens bare

Stars reflect in the ocean's deep gaze
Where past and present intertwine, they blaze
Gentle tides cleanse the sorrow we keep
Offering solace, a promise to keep

Notations on Shore

Waves compose music, a symphony grand
Each note a kiss upon the golden sand
Birds join in with harmonies pure
Nature's orchestra, an eternal allure

Ripples write stories on the ocean's face
Ephemeral scripts of transient grace
Pebbles scatter like thoughts in the mind
In this symphony, serenity we find

Wind chimes resonate, the song of the shore
Moments and melodies, forevermore
In this cadence, our hearts find their beat
Unified in nature's endless suite

Wind-Tousled Imprints

In the embrace of a relentless gale
Sand shifts and dances, leaving a trail
Each breeze a whisper, a tale to be told
In the language of freedom bold

Dunes curve, reshaped by unseen hands
Marking the passage of time with strands
Footprints fade, but their story remains
Amidst the wind, echoing through plains

Grass sways softly, a murmured retreat
Earth and sky in harmony complete
Imprints linger, transient yet anew
Wind-carved memories, forever true

Chasing the Breeze

With every gust, aspirations take flight
Dreams pursue the wind, reaching new height
Leaves flutter, a dance both wild and free
In this chase, boundless possibility

Hair tousled, skin kissed by the breeze
Life awakens in moments like these
Over hills and through the valleys wide
We follow the whispers, our guide

Eyes closed, hearts open to the song
In nature's rhythm, we belong
Through the winds, our souls find ease
Forever chasing the fleeting breeze

Wanderers' Trace

Along the winding paths we tread,
Through forests dense and skies so wide,
Where dreams and whispers gently lead,
In nature's arms, our hearts confide.

Mountains high and valleys deep,
With every step we lay our claim,
On journeys vast where shadows sleep,
Bound together, free from shame.

In meadows draped in twilight's hue,
Whispered winds, the soul's embrace,
Footprints fade, yet we renew,
In wanderers' trace, our boundless grace.

Ephemeral Steps

Moments fleeting, like morning dew,
Gathered softly on blades of grass,
Each step we take, a story new,
In the breath of dawn, we softly pass.

Through corridors of time we slip,
Ephemeral steps, a fleeting dance,
With gentle hearts and softened grip,
We seize the day, by happenstance.

In twilight's calm, our shadows blend,
Whispered promises, moonlight beams,
Ephemeral steps, until the end,
We journey forth on golden dreams.

Gone with the Tide

Beneath the azure sky so vast,
Dance the waves of time's embrace,
Memories anchored in the past,
Gone with the tide, we leave no trace.

Silent whispers of the sea,
Echoes of what once did strive,
Bound as one yet wild and free,
In the ebbing flow, we come alive.

From shore to shore, the waters call,
Secrets held within their glide,
Ever moving, yet we fall,
Gone with the tide, on life's tide.

Shoreline Whispers

On the shoreline, whispers meet,
Soft and tender, calm as night,
Waves embrace in rhythmic beat,
Stars above their watchful light.

Footprints in the sand we leave,
Stories told in every grain,
As the tides both give and heave,
Whispers weave through joy and pain.

Morning dawns, horizon bright,
Shoreline whispers call anew,
Filling hearts with pure delight,
In each wave, a promise true.

Resonance on the Strand

Waves crash upon the silent shore
Eternal dance, forevermore
Moonlight whispers ancient lore
In the night, the spirits soar

Footprints trace along the sand
Ephemeral marks by nature planned
Echoes ring where lovers stand
In this transient, timeless land

Shells and stones, forgotten dreams
Collecting fragments, mystery seems
Beneath the starlit, silver beams
The ocean's voice in midnight streams

Ebb and Imprint

The tide pulls back, a gentle sigh
Leaving treasures, driftwood dry
Stories written in the sky
We ponder them with wonder, why?

Our steps their mark in wet ground leave
Fleeting moments, do not grieve
For life, like tides, will soon retrieve
New paths, new dreams we dare conceive

The sun sets low, horizon's fire
Burning with ancient desire
All things transient, we aspire
To find our place, hearts lifted higher

Seashore Legacy

Ancient whispers in the breeze
Oceans sing of memories
Of far-off lands, stormy seas
Their legacy in constant tease

Footprints fading in the sand
Children building dreams by hand
By morning light and evening grand
The future cast, a fleeting strand

Driftwood tales and sailor's myths
Oceans gifting solace fifths
Time a wave that always shifts
Leaving legacies in drifts

By the Water's Edge

Shadows lengthen, day is done
By the water's edge, we've won
Moments captured, every one
Beneath the sky, the setting sun

Pebbles skipping, laughter's song
Ripples echoing, soft and long
By the shore where hearts belong
Nature's chorus, pure and strong

In the stillness, peace we find
Ocean vast, both free and kind
Reflections of the heart and mind
By the water's edge, entwined

Mirage and Memory

In a desert warm and wide,
Mirages play tricks on the eye,
Dunes stretching far and wide,
Blurring dreams where they lie.

Old memories rise in the heat,
Ghosts of times once sweet,
Waves of heat beneath my feet,
Distort the truths we greet.

Illusions of water beckon me,
Oasis just out of reach,
Mirage and memory, a sea,
In the sands they each beseech.

Time and vision intertwine,
Fables lost to sand and brine,
What was real, what was thine,
Mirage and memory combine.

Shadows dance in desert lore,
Reminders of what's come before,
In the arid land, a silent roar,
Mirage and memory explore.

Erosion and Echoes

Waves crash upon the shore,
In an endless, rhythmic chore,
Erosion whispers evermore,
Shaping cliffs to their core.

Mountains wear their ancient scars,
Etched by elements from afar,
Erosion's touch, a soft memoir,
Carving tales beneath the stars.

Echoes of the ocean's voice,
Songs of past that now rejoice,
Through the winds they find their choice,
Resonating, void of noise.

Rivers etch their winding tales,
Through valleys, stones, and trails,
Erosion carries what prevails,
Leaving whispers in the gales.

Sand and rock in constant dance,
Nature's ever-changing trance,
Erosion's gentle, patient stance,
Echoes of a timeless romance.

Sand Symphony

Golden grains beneath my toes,
A symphony where the ocean flows,
The whispers of the breezes show,
Melodies the earth bestows.

Seashells sing a silent tune,
Underneath the silver moon,
Ebb and flow from noon to noon,
Nature's song, a timeless boon.

Dunes that shift in gentle sway,
Compose a chorus in the bay,
Wind and wave in soft array,
Notes that dance in light's display.

Crabs that scuttle, birds that cry,
Add their voices to the sky,
In this world where spirits fly,
A harmony we can't deny.

Sand Symphony in endless play,
Music found in each new day,
In the dance of earth and spray,
Songs of time that never fade.

Journeys of the Coastline

Footprints on a sandy shore,
Stories written by the core,
Journeys that were lived before,
Etched in time, forevermore.

Cliffs that guard the ocean's edge,
Bound by a solemn pledge,
To hold secrets in their wedge,
Of every oath and every dredge.

Seagulls soar with tales to tell,
Of coastal paths where dreams dwell,
In their wings, the memories swell,
Of places where the waves rebel.

Sunsets paint the sky in hues,
Marking paths for you to choose,
Journeys seen in reds and blues,
Of ancient lands and morning dews.

In the heart where waters meet,
Journeys of the shoreline greet,
With every step, the past we'll meet,
On life's ever-winding beat.

Imprints of Ephemeral Journeys

Footprints fade in morning dew,
Whispers of a distant crew.
Paths once crossed, now lost anew,
Ever shifting, time's encore view.

Stars above, a guiding light,
Fleeting shadows in the night.
Chasing dreams on wings of flight,
Fading softly out of sight.

Moments passed with joy and tears,
Mark the passing of the years.
Echoes blend in silent cheers,
Memory's thread that disappears.

Along the way, brief imprints stay,
In hearts where wanderers lay,
Marking once an olden day,
Before time sweeps all away.

Journey's end, a new commence,
Life's ephemeral dance,
Bound by interwoven sense,
Towards tomorrow's chance.

Stories Beneath the Dunes

Beneath the golden sands they lie,
Whispers of the ages nigh.
Tales of time and quests gone by,
Hidden where the dunes do sigh.

Ancient trails in grains conceal,
Mysteries time won't reveal.
Shadows of a past surreal,
In the silent, shifting zeal.

Windswept whispers softly tell,
Silent stories cast their spell.
Of love, of loss, of rising swell,
In the heart's deep timeless well.

Footsteps lost in desert's breath,
Erase the paths with silent stealth.
Leaving scarce a trace or wealth,
Of those who walked with life and health.

In the sands, the stories sleep,
Guarded secrets buried deep.
Waiting for the eyes that peep,
To find the tales the winds do keep.

Transient Trails by the Sea

Waves that kiss the golden shore,
Leave behind and take once more.
Transient trails of dreams galore,
Footsteps washed as tides explore.

Shells that whisper tales of yore,
Ebbing tides forever more.
Marks that blend and swirl the core,
Of stories lost in ocean's roar.

Gulls that call and breezes play,
Mark the paths that wash away.
Transient trails in fleeting stay,
Moments lived in endless sway.

Upon the sands, a love is traced,
Only for the sea to taste.
Fleeting, fragile, soon erased,
By the waves in gentle haste.

Yet as the sea breathes in and out,
New trails form with every bout.
Transient, though without a doubt,
Life's own hymn in waves that shout.

Serenity in Each Step

With each step, a breath anew,
Infinite peace comes into view.
Moments still, the sky so blue,
Whispering winds, a tranquil cue.

Footfalls soft on earthen lane,
Heartbeats sync with nature's vein.
Calm flows gently through the plain,
In the quiet, none remain.

Blossoms nod in silent grace,
Leaves that dance in still embrace.
Each small step, a slower pace,
Finds serenity's warm space.

Paths that twist through meadows wide,
Echo with the footfalls' stride.
Each calm step, in peace abide,
Life's calm rhythm as its guide.

In each step, a world does bloom,
Silent as the twilight's gloom.
Serenity in nature's room,
Heals the heart and soothes the plume.

Coastal Narratives

Waves whisper on the shore,
Salt-kissed breezes roar.
Footprints fade from sight,
In the silver twilight.

Pebbles glint, stories untold,
Legends buried in grains of gold.
Ships sail past horizons vast,
Leaving echoes of the past.

Lighthouses guard with light,
Against the dark of night.
Seagulls call from above,
An ode to oceans they love.

Tides rise, embrace land,
A timeless dance, hand in hand.
Shells cast upon the strand,
Gems from Neptune's band.

Sailors speak of ancient lore,
Each tale a cherished core.
Under stars, beside the sea,
Bound to nature's decree.

Silent Passageways

Shadows drape the hollow lanes,
Silent whispers cast no chains.
Moonlight spills on cobblestones,
Where solitude softly moans.

Lanterns flicker, ghosts explore,
Echoes linger evermore.
Silence holds these paths in thrall,
Where the stars at nightfall call.

Locks rust on gates that guard,
Memories stand on shattered shards.
Every step on ancient ground,
Resonates a haunting sound.

Dew-kissed moss in moonlit glow,
Hides the tales we'll never know.
Secret paths among the trees,
Sigh with every passing breeze.

Footfalls in the dusky air,
Trace the journey, unaware.
Midnight hearts, they wander by,
Underneath the silent sky.

Shorebound Impressions

Waves sketch tales upon the sand,
With a fleeting, gentle hand.
Sunrise paints the world anew,
In a palette wide of hue.

Seashells lay in scattered art,
Each one crafted with a heart.
Driftwood whispers tales of yore,
On this ever-changing shore.

Sandcastles rise by children's dreams,
Crabs and gulls in playful schemes.
The maritime winds, a constant song,
As the surf rolls waves along.

Beach grass sways with rhythms pure,
Nature's dance, both wild and sure.
Footprints weave a transient track,
Of those who may not soon come back.

Sunsets bathe the coastal line,
In colors rich, a scene divine.
A symphony where waves and tide,
Sing the shore's eternal guide.

Tales along the Coast

Mermaids sing in evening light,
Drawing sailors through the night.
Their voices weave a magic tale,
On the sea's eternal trail.

Cliffs stand tall with rugged pride,
Guarding stories that they hide.
Every wave against the stone,
Writes a history unknown.

Harbors cradle ships at rest,
Peaceful in the twilight's nest.
Fisher folk with nets and gear,
Speak of days both far and near.

Wind carries whispers wide,
Of adventures out on tide.
Each breeze tells of love and loss,
Painted on the ocean's gloss.

Stars blink out their old refrain,
Over waters that remain.
Tales of yore and dreams untamed,
By the coastline's hearts proclaimed.

Foundations in the Tideline

Footprints mingled with ocean's breath,
Tracing stories beneath the crest.
Each wave whispers secrets frail,
Of ancient mariners, in every tale.

Pebbled shores, a history sown,
In the sand where dreams are thrown.
Against the tides, our hopes stand,
Eroded slowly by nature's hand.

Driftwood castles rise and fall,
Symbol of impermanence to all.
In the dance of moon and sea,
Foundations blur, spirits flee.

Twilight grazes the water's edge,
While stars promise every pledge.
Boundless, the horizon's glow,
On tides that endlessly flow.

Murmurs of the deep intertwine,
With whispered thoughts, yours and mine.
Foundations built, soon replaced,
In the eternal, sea's embrace.

Through Sand and Time

Grains of wisdom, passage of years,
Each one tells of laughter and tears.
Through glistening dunes, we wander far,
Beneath the sun, beneath the stars.

Eons whisper to the sky,
In the silence where echoes lie.
Every step a memory framed,
In a canvas, eternally named.

Beneath our feet, dreams reside,
Shifting sands, the world wide.
Time's river, in silent streams,
Flows between our whispered dreams.

In the desert's heartbeat, we find
Traces of ancient humankind.
Stories etched in nature's art,
We are but part and yet apart.

As sunsets blaze in fiery shade,
And stars emerge where shadows played,
Through sand and time, we humbly trace
The fleeting dance of our embrace.

Patrick's Journey

Under skies both dark and bright,
Patrick wanders through the night.
Cloaked in dreams and visions rare,
He seeks a path with tender care.

Mountains rise and valleys fall,
Nature answers every call.
Patrick's heart, a compass guided,
By the stars that have resided.

Through forests dense and rivers wide,
Across the plains, horizons wide,
Patrick's footsteps echo true,
With every dawn, a world anew.

In his quest, he finds his soul,
A tapestry that time unrolls.
Journey's end or journey's start,
It's the road that shapes the heart.

Under moon and sun's embrace,
Patrick finds his destined place.
Every trail and road he sees,
Leads him closer to his peace.

Elusive Strides

Chasing shadows in twilight's grace,
Elusive strides in the night we trace.
Through the veil of dawn's embrace,
Whispered dreams we dare to chase.

Footprints fleeting in the sand,
Moments slip through our hands.
With every step, a path unwinds,
Sentences lost between the lines.

Silent echoes on the breeze,
Carry tales of distant seas.
Strides that vanish with the light,
Merge with the endless night.

Ephemeral yet bold and strong,
Strides of those who wander long.
In the night, beneath the stars,
Hope and memory spars.

Through every dusk and every dawn,
We walk the paths where dreams are drawn.
Elusive strides, forever more,
Tracing lives, an endless lore.

Moving Through the Mirage

Whispers of a desert breeze
Secrets buried in the sand
Shadows dance with fleeting ease
Lost in paths the heart has planned

Oases shimmer, transient lies
Mirages gleam, the mind deceives
In this land where silence sighs
Hope like grains through fingers leaves

Sunset bleeds across the dunes
Stars refrain from endless night
Dreams like ancient, haunting tunes
Glimmers fade beyond our sight

Horizon blurs, a blinding glow
Footprints traced in golden dust
Journeys more than we will know
Faith in wander, bound by trust

Voices fade as echoes clear
Desert keeps its mystic hold
Truths unveiled, a world austere
Magic in the vast untold

Tales of the Tides

Waves that speak in rhythmic lore
Stories held within their swell
Secrets from a distant shore
In their rise and fall, they tell

Moonlit whispers guide their dance
Tales of love and fleeting time
In their ceaseless, swaying trance
Burdened truths and lies combined

Ships lost in the ocean's song
Memories of tempests past
In the swirling depths belong
Dreams and shadows miscast

Sailors weave their yarns of old
Legends born of brine and foam
Mysteries the tides withhold
Far from hearth and driftwood home

Every crest and every trough
Echoes of the vast unknown
In their pull, we're led aloft
Into stories overthrown

Strolls by the Sea's Edge

Footsteps traced in morning's light
Whispers of the breaking dawn
Sea and sky in hues unite
Promise of a day reborn

Gulls cry out their strange allure
Wings embrace the salty air
On the shore, dreams feel so pure
Daylight's touch, beyond compare

Pebbles washed by endless waves
Sculpted smooth, by time refined
Memories that ocean saves
Fragments of a distant mind

Walking paths where waters kiss
Shores that paint a tale of old
In each step, a fleeting bliss
Nature's secrets unfold

Horizons meet in tranquil blend
Soul and sea as one align
At the edge, here moments lend
Glimpses of the grand design

Ephemeral Shorelines

Fading prints on evening sands
Time's soft touch in twilight hues
Whispers of far-distant lands
Echoes gentle in the muse

Tides retreat, then surge anew
Moments lost, forever gone
In their cycle, skies imbue
Colors of the dusk and dawn

Memories like shells abide
Polished by the endless sea
In their shapes and curves reside
Stories of infinity

As the shadows lengthen, grow
Boundaries blur in soft repose
Ephemeral, the world we know
Fleeting as the daylight goes

Standing where the waters gleam
Edge between the now and then
In this transitory dream
Catch the whispers of the wren

Dreams in Drift

In fields of gold my dreams take flight,
Stars are born in the silent night.
Upon the breeze, my hopes do soar,
To lands unseen, forevermore.

A bridge of light across the sky,
Links the heartlines, you and I.
With every pulse, a wish comes true,
In dreams, old paths are made anew.

Whispers call through twilight's veil,
Mysteries in the moonlight pale.
Footsteps fade on forgotten clay,
But dreams in drift, they find their way.

In slumber's grasp and shadowed mind,
Boundless visions, unconfined.
Echoes of a life profound,
In dreams, our spirit shall be found.

Imprints on the Shoreline

Steps are softened by the tide,
Footprints fade where memories hide.
Each grain of sand a story told,
Imprints on the shoreline bold.

Waves embrace the earth's great chest,
Smoothing all that's once been stressed.
Ancient echoes whisper low,
Secrets in the undertow.

The ocean's breath, a lullaby,
Sings to stars in moonlit sky.
We leave our mark, yet soon it flees,
Woven in with shifting seas.

The waters dance in silvered light,
Receding dreams from darkest night.
Each mark we make, though swift erased,
In hearts it lingers, ever traced.

Echoes by the Ocean

Beneath the azure heavens clear,
The ocean whispers in my ear.
A tale of ages long since past,
Echoes by the ocean vast.

The waves that kiss the sandy shore,
Bring tales of lands and loves of yore.
A haunting song of distant climes,
Resonates through seas and times.

The heartbeats blend with rhythmic tide,
Whispers of a world so wide.
In every crash, a voice is found,
Announcing secrets most profound.

Under the ever-watchful gaze,
Of sun and moon in bright displays.
The ocean keeps its endless lore,
Echoes we feel forevermore.

Whispers of the Beach

Beneath the sun's embrace, we lie,
Where sea meets sky and seagulls cry.
Soft whispers on the sandy reach,
Enchanting songs, the beach beseech.

Driftwood tales and seagrass play,
In melodies of yesterday.
Each shell a vessel, tale inside,
Of where the ocean's heart resides.

The breeze entwines with ancient lore,
Recounted on the sandy shore.
In quiet murmurs, waves impart,
Timeless truths to open hearts.

As sun descends in fiery sleep,
In shadows, dreams and whispers seep.
Each grain of sand a promise made,
At twilight, memories won't fade.

Traces in the Granules

Whispers on the desert's breeze
Shift the sands with subtle ease
Time leaves marks in endless ways
Footprints linger, then erase

Granules glow in sunlight's sweep
Memories in dunes so deep
Patterns drawn by nature's play
Fleeting glimpses of the day

In the night, the stars align
Grains reflect their twinkling sign
Histories in silence tell
Of places where the shadows dwell

Footsteps fade, but leave a trace
In the granules find their place
Ephemeral, yet so defined
In the sands of time, we find

Whispers carried, dark and light
Dancing through the day and night
In each granule, life's embrace
Marking paths that we retrace

Memory's Pathway

Winding through the forest green
Echoes of where we have been
Leaves crunch soft beneath our feet
Recollections bittersweet

Sunlight filters through the trees
Gentle whispers in the breeze
Years have marked the paths we trod
Steps in sync with nature's nod

Time flows like the river's bend
Memory's path will never end
Moments captured, feelings sway
Guiding us along the way

Beneath the canopy, we find
Echoes of what's left behind
Shadows dance as if to say
Memories never fade away

In the pathways, truth revealed
Scars and joys in time congealed
Every turn a testament
Tracing life where we have went

Seaside Remnants

Waves caress the sandy shore
Whispers of the ocean's lore
Seashells speak in silent tones
Stories etched in ancient stones

Tides that ebb and tides that flow
Mark the passage, ebb and grow
Each arrival, each retreat
Marks the rhythm, pure and fleet

Footprints trace a fleeting tale
Lost beneath the moon's soft pale
As the water's edge recedes
Echoes of our own misdeeds

Driftwood whispers secrets old
Held in patterns, weathered bold
In the silence, waves bestow
Seaside remnants ebb and flow

On the shore, the winds will guide
Memories of the changing tide
Every crest and every fall
Whispers faint, but heard by all

Silent Walks by the Tide

Strolling where the waves collide
Silent walks by the tide
Night unfolds, the stars ignite
Guiding steps in gentle light

Salt-kissed air and water's song
Echoing the shore along
In the quiet, hearts converse
With the sea as their universe

Footsteps blend with whispered breeze
Hushed by endless, rolling seas
In the space where dreams reside
Silent walks by the tide

Moon's reflection gently sways
Casting light on twilight's gaze
In the calm, our souls confide
Silent walks by the tide

Boundless, wide, the ocean's lore
Answers hidden on the shore
In each wave, a secret hides
Silent walks by the tide

Fleeting Impressions

A whisper in the morning light
Soft echoes of the dawn's delight
Shadows dance, then fade away
Impressions made, but none will stay

Ephemeral, the twilight sands
Falling through our grasping hands
Moments shift, like drifting seas
Gone before we feel the breeze

An artist's stroke, a poet's rhyme
Capturing the fleeting time
Briefly there, like morning mist
Evanescent as a kiss

Ghostly trails on paths we've crossed
Lingering yet forever lost
Echoes of a silent call
Fleeting impressions, that is all

In the end, we hold but air
Shimmering dreams beyond compare
Transient, as a songbird's tune
Vanishing beneath the moon

Pathways of Time

On pathways marked by ancient lore
We tread where countless feet explore
From dawn to dusk, throughout the years
Tracing time with hopes and fears

Each step we take, in shadow cast
Becomes a tie to moments past
An echo of what used to be
A glimpse into our history

Journey forth through endless streams
Following paths of fleeting dreams
The present yields to past designs
Woven into time's lifelines

Cobblestones of memory pave
The roads we travel, bold or brave
Etching tales in silent stone
Pathways where our stories hone

Through the fog of future's haze
We walk the trails of bygone days
Each moment, a footprint laid
On pathways of time, unafraid

Transitory Trails

Beneath the sky's expansive dome
We wander trails far from home
In the footsteps of the past
Hoping that the journey lasts

Through forests deep and valleys wide
We find our way, without a guide
Each moment, a fleeting phase
Transitory in its gaze

The winds of change around us blow
Shifting sands where e'er we go
Paths we walk are seldom straight
Twisting like the threads of fate

A transient dance, our earthly stay
Moving forward, come what may
Marking trails with fleeting prints
Leaving whispers, subtle hints

In the end, no trail remains
Lost in time's unyielding chains
We wander on through life's grand wails
On countless, transitory trails

Eternal Marks

On landscapes vast, our deeds inscribe
In timeless realms, our stories thrive
Each sentence carved, an endless spark
Leaving in the world, eternal marks

With every life, a line is drawn
A testament to days long gone
In hearts and minds our presence stays
Living on through endless days

The hands of time, they gently trace
The lines upon our weathered face
Memories that never fade
In the legacy we've laid

As stars in distant skies ignite
Our spirits soar, in boundless flight
Through darkness, light shall found its way
Eternal marks, in break of day

Though we may fade, our essence bides
In whispers on the shifting tides
For in each act, each loving arc
We leave behind eternal marks

Wind-written Trails

In fields where whispers go astray,
The winds inscribe their fleeting tale,
On leaves and grass, they lightly lay,
A story told in gentle gale.

From mountaintops to valleys deep,
Their fingers trace the earth's soft face,
Composing songs the wild will keep,
In notes of quiet, spectral grace.

At dusk, the twilight lends its ink,
Stars witness as the breezes scribe,
A message lost within the brink,
Of nature's vast, untamed tribe.

Eternal movements, never still,
They craft a prose of airy might,
Each gust a line, to bend or fill,
The canvas of the endless night.

So listen well, where zephyrs roam,
In meadows, where their spirits sail,
For there you'll find, in nature's poem,
The wind's soft-spoken, whispered trail.

Vanishing Narratives

The pages linger, thin as breath,
With words that fade like evening mist,
A chronicle of whispered death,
In tomes that time has gently kissed.

Ghosts of tales once brightly spun,
Now drift in shadows, pale and thin,
A tapestry undone, unspun,
Where moonlight weaves its phantom spin.

Old echoes haunt the memory,
Of stories lost to shifting sands,
Their whispers like a mournful plea,
In languages of distant lands.

Each fleeting word, a firefly,
In twilight's deep, elusive glow,
They flicker briefly, then they die,
Into the void, where lost things go.

Yet somewhere in the silent night,
Their essence breathes, though shadows fall,
Vanishing narratives take flight,
In dreams, where they are free to call.

Tidal Glyphs

Upon the shore where oceans sigh,
The waves inscribe their mystic signs,
In fluid scripts where secrets lie,
Etched softly on the coastal lines.

The sand, a canvas born anew,
With each embrace of briny hand,
A language known by but a few,
Translates the sea's unspoken plan.

In symbols shaped by lunar tides,
The ocean writes its ancient lore,
Of hidden depths and shifting rides,
That speak of what's been seen before.

These glyphs, ephemeral and grand,
Erase as quickly as they're writ,
By waters bound to sweep the sand,
In verses lost where silence knits.

Yet as each wave retreats once more,
It leaves behind a fleeting trace,
A tidal glyph upon the shore,
A moment's mark on nature's face.

Saltwater Echoes

Beneath the waves where silence sings,
Lie echoes of a distant past,
They resonate in hidden springs,
And memories in currents cast.

The ocean's voice, a mournful sound,
Carries whispers of forgotten lore,
From sunken ships and treasures found,
To secrets lost along the shore.

Each ripple holds a story's hue,
In saltwater where time once flowed,
Reflecting skies of sea-born blue,
In depths where ancient voices rode.

Through coral reefs and seagrass beds,
The echoes wend their solemn path,
Weaving tapestries of reds,
And blues in watery, wondrous math.

So listen close, where tides converge,
In the vast embrace where currents glow,
To saltwater echoes as they surge,
With tales the deep alone can show.

Echoes on the Shore

Beneath the sky, where waves do dance,
Sunset colors in a vibrant trance,
Shells whisper tales of distant lands,
In melody, with shifting sands.

Gulls cry high, in ocean's roar,
Footsteps mingled with days of yore,
Time leaves traces, soft yet pure,
Echoes linger on the shore.

Castles built with hopes and dreams,
Tides will wash them, so it seems,
Yet in hearts, they will endure,
Stories crafted, ever sure.

Moonlight weaves, a satin thread,
Paths of memory, where they tread,
Whispers faint, forevermore,
Echoes calling from the shore.

Love and loss, in waves embraced,
Moments fleeting, none erased,
Hearken to the ocean's lore,
Echoes singing on the shore.

Whispers of Tomorrow

In dawn's embrace, a fresh start gleams,
Tomorrow's whispers fill our dreams,
Hope takes flight on fragile wings,
Future's promise, softly sings.

Paths ahead, both known and new,
Choices shaping what we do,
Each breath drawn, a silent vow,
In whispers of tomorrow, now.

Stars align in twilight's grace,
Lighting up our destined place,
Voices call from future days,
Guiding us through unknown maze.

Courage found in moments still,
Strength in heart, a steadfast will,
Step by step, we cast aside,
Doubts and fears, no longer hide.

Morning breaks with golden hue,
Dreams relived, each one renewed,
In whispers, future finds its way,
To shape our every coming day.

Silent Trails

Winding paths through forests deep,
Where ancient trees their secrets keep,
Footsteps fall on mossy ground,
In silence, nature's voice is found.

Shadows play beneath the leaves,
Whispering winds in autumn's eves,
Softly tread where none have been,
Silent trails, a world unseen.

Echoes of a bygone age,
History caught in nature's page,
Listen close to roots and vines,
Stories told in silent signs.

Streams that babble, stones that stand,
Silent witnesses of the land,
Every turn a mystery,
Silent trails in revelry.

Through the woods and o'er the hill,
Follow trails that call us still,
In the hush of evening's glow,
Silent secrets, ever flow.

Memories in the Grains

Each grain of sand, a tale of yore,
Moments lost on time's vast shore,
Whispers linger, soft and keen,
Memories in the grains unseen.

Eyes that glance at sunsets past,
Hold in them, a spell that's cast,
Summer's laughter, winter's breeze,
Captured in the grains with ease.

Footprints fade but not the love,
Sentiments like stars above,
Treasure found where sands unfurl,
In every boy and every girl.

Stories told by campfire bright,
Echoes of our youthful light,
Fragments held in grains of time,
Memories in silent rhyme.

Seasons change and yet remain,
Timeless in each tiny grain,
Shifting through the hands once more,
Memories in sands of yore.

Shifting Ground Underfoot

Beneath the soles, the earth does weave
An ever-changing tapestry,
Patterns lost in ancient lore,
Mysteries to be explored.

Geos whisper secrets deep,
Rooted in the slumbers keep,
Soil and stone, both old and new,
Shift to form a newfound view.

Each step taken, cautious tread,
Where past and present are both led,
Through the landscape's heaving breath,
Dancing on the edge of myth.

Chaos melds with nature's hand,
Underfoot we understand,
Every shift's an echo loud,
In the silence nature's proud.

Feet leave traces where they roam,
Marking realms to call their own,
Ground that moves with quiet grace,
A tale of change within this place.

Trailblazing in the Sand

Paths are lost where dunes do rise,
Sculpted by the windy skies,
Footsteps fade to time's command,
Etched but briefly in the sand.

Sunburnt hues and golden glows,
Mark the ways a traveler goes,
Yet each print's a fleeting trace,
In the desert's vast embrace.

Lonely wind, a whispered guide,
Through the grains where secrets hide,
Every step a quest unplanned,
Trailblazing in the sand.

Beneath the stars, the desert shifts,
A sea of dreams, and memory drifts,
Ever transient, grains of old,
In the warmth of day's unfold.

Bound by none, the path renews,
As trailblazers chase the views,
In the sand where moments blend,
Journey's truth, no clear end.

Whispers of the Coast

The ocean's breath, a tranquil sigh,
Seagulls paint the azure sky,
Tides converse in rhythmic tone,
Songs of shores, a world unknown.

Pebbles tell of journeys grand,
Rolled and shaped by nature's hand,
Each a story, time does boast,
Written in whispers of the coast.

Salt-kissed breeze on skin so fair,
Carries dreams beyond compare,
Tempests, calm, they both array,
The coast is where the heart does sway.

Ebb and flow, the dance of waves,
Secrets kept in coral caves,
Whispers soft of fish and shell,
Of ancient tales they long to tell.

As twilight falls, the coastal sound,
Lingers as the night surrounds,
In the blend of dusk and ghost,
One hears the whispers of the coast.

Impermanent Paths

Steps engraved in dew-soaked grass,
Mornings wane, their legacies pass,
Trails are made, then fade away,
In the light of breaking day.

The forest floor, a canvas vast,
Each imprint subtle, none to last,
Leaves fall, covering the track,
Paths once walked, now turning back.

Winter snows will sweep them clean,
Blanket white replaces green,
Impermanent paths they drift,
Silent in their sacred shift.

Moonlit nights, where shadows play,
Mark the routes that lead astray,
Echoes of the steps once bold,
Dissipate to tales untold.

Wanderers in time we are,
Leaving marks both near and far,
Tracing maps of fleeting kind,
Etched in memory, undefined.

Journey into Dunes

Through golden waves of sunlit dunes,
Our shadows trace a dance of runes.
The wind, a whisper, sings a tune,
In desert's quiet afternoon.

Footprints tell a tale untold,
Where dreams weave into stories bold.
The sands, they shift, a saga spun,
Of journeys slowed, of races won.

Time stands still under sky so vast,
The desert's secrets ever last.
In every grain, a history cast,
Of future paths and echoes past.

The heat, a lover's warm embrace,
Leaves crimson kisses on our face.
The dunes, they rise, a wavy lace,
A sculpted dance in arid space.

Stars will light night's velvet dome,
The dunes will sleep, as shadows roam.
Our hearts find peace, our souls a home,
In desert's arms, no need to roam.

Summertime Stories

Under sun's caress, gentle and bright,
Children play from dawn till night.
The breeze sings tales of pure delight,
Of summer's joy and endless flight.

Picnics spread on emerald ground,
Laughter flows, a joyous sound.
In each small story, magic found,
Where hearts and hopes are tightly bound.

The ocean's kiss, a cool embrace,
Waves dance and shimmer, keeping pace.
In the sand, our dreams we trace,
Lost in summer's gentle grace.

Fireflies twinkle in twilight's shade,
Nature's lanterns softly played.
Stories old and new are made,
In summer's golden serenade.

As stars awaken in the sky,
Goodbyes are said with happy sigh.
Summertime whispers never die,
They live forever in a child's eye.

Legends in Sand

Ancient tales in grains of sand,
Passed down through time by wind's soft hand.
Heroes bold and quests so grand,
Echoed in this vast, dry land.

Kingdoms rose and poets sung,
Battles fought, their banners hung.
Each legend whispered, softly strung,
In desert's silence, ever young.

The sun, a witness to each tale,
No parchment needs, no ink that's pale.
In shifting dunes, where shadows veil,
We find where myth and truth congeal.

Camels tread where pharaohs tread,
Upon the sands where gods have bled.
Mysteries wrapped in golden thread,
In desert's heart, our stories spread.

So when night falls and stars convene,
Remember tales once lost, unseen.
In desert's breath, a past serene,
Legends in sand, a timeless dream.

Glossy Trails

Morning dew on spider veins,
Glitters bright on grassy plains.
Nature writes in liquid chains,
Stories set in glossy frames.

Forest paths gleam wet with rain,
Whispers soft in each refrain.
Our steps leave marks, a gentle strain,
Tracing life through wood's domain.

River's song, a silvered tune,
Underneath the tender moon.
Glossy trails will vanish soon,
In light of day, a fleeting boon.

Butterfly wings behold the glow,
Reflect the sun in beauty's show.
Tales are told in whispers low,
Where glossy trails of wonder flow.

In nature's book, each trail unfurled,
A shiny path through mystic world.
Glossy trails, our lives they swirl,
In this bright, enchanted whirl.

Azure Borders

Across the vast, unending seas,
Where sky meets the horizon's gleam,
A dance of waves with endless ease,
Whispers of an eternal dream.

Sunlight kisses water's edge,
Diamond sparkles on a quay,
Waves recite an ocean pledge,
Boundless blue in wild array.

Seagulls trace the open air,
Feathers blending with the sky,
A symphony without compare,
Echoes of a distant sigh.

Clouds adrift in cotton grace,
Reflect in waters deep and clear,
Nature holds an old embrace,
An azure tale both far and near.

Time dissolves in boundless blue,
No end, no start within this scene,
A borderless and gentle hue,
Wraps the world in a serene sheen.

Tranquil Traces

In silent woods where shadows play,
Soft whispers dance among the trees,
The rustle of the leaves in sway,
Carries tales on tranquil breeze.

Mossy paths in twilight's glow,
Guide the way through ancient pines,
Steps are light, and hearts beat slow,
In quiet realms where peace aligns.

Streams that murmur, soft and clear,
Weave through rocks with gentle grace,
Nature's song, so faint yet near,
Leaves behind a tranquil trace.

Birds in hush, their wings at rest,
Blanket skies with gentle flight,
In this haven, spirits blessed,
Find their solace in the night.

Underneath the moon's embrace,
Dreams take form in silver light,
Soft and quiet, the wood's face,
Wears a calm that feels just right.

Echoes of Pebbles

On shores where tiny pebbles lie,
Each one tells a story, light,
Of tides that kiss them with a sigh,
In the calm of moonlit night.

Waves that whisper, secrets keep,
Rolling in with gentle grace,
Pebbles smooth from ocean's sweep,
Nature's touch leaves no trace.

Footprints linger for a while,
Paws of creatures, marks of men,
Soon erased by ocean's smile,
Gone, but echoes breathe again.

Children's laughter fills the air,
Pebbles tossed with carefree might,
Ripples dancing, unaware,
Of the timeless, fleeting flight.

Memories on shorelines cast,
Echoes drift in rhythmic sound,
Pebbles bear a silent past,
In their forms, life's cycles found.

Coastal Whispers

Where land and sea in union meet,
Waves caress the sandy shore,
A melody, both soft and sweet,
Whispers of the ocean's lore.

Palm trees sway in rhythm's song,
Lulled by breezes from the west,
Seabirds join and sing along,
Nature's choir, the very best.

Sailboats drift with gentle ease,
Cutting through the salty spray,
Canvas kissed by playful breeze,
As the sun concludes its day.

Bonfires burn with golden glow,
Casting warmth on faces dear,
Stories shared while embers show,
Waves' soft whispers draw them near.

Moonlight dances on the tide,
Mimics stars in night's embrace,
Coastal whispers gently bide,
Eternal, in their sacred space.

Transient Patterns

Footsteps trace a fleeting trail,
Across the sands so wide and pale,
Echoes whisper, soft and frail,
In transient patterns, we sail.

Waves caress the shifting shore,
Erasing marks of days before,
Moments caught in nature's lore,
Transient patterns evermore.

The wind, it sings a fleeting song,
Through trees that sway, to night belong,
In their dance, our hearts prolong,
Patterns transient, right or wrong.

Stars above, they twinkle bright,
Guiding us through dark of night,
In their glow, a transient light,
Patterns fade with morning's sight.

Life, a waltz on time's own stage,
Chapters turning, page by page,
Transient patterns, they engage,
Writing stories, age to age.

Sands of Yesterday

In the sands of yesterday,
Memories buried, far away,
Time's own whispers softly say,
Leave behind, yet do not stray.

Footprints lead through desert's span,
Echoes of what once began,
In their trace, the tales of man,
Lost in sands where dreams outran.

Dunes arise, then softly fall,
Silent witness to it all,
In their curves, a distant call,
Of the days we can't recall.

Sunsets paint the sky in gold,
Stories of the past retold,
In the sands, both young and old,
Tales of love, and lives of bold.

Through the sands of yesterday,
Hope remains, come what may,
In their grains, dreams will stay,
Guiding us, our hearts' relay.

Ephemeral Journeys

On ephemeral journeys we embark,
Through the light and through the dark,
Ghostly trails where shadows park,
Navigating life's bizarre arc.

Whispers of the past we chase,
In the wind, a fleeting grace,
Ephemeral journeys, life's swift pace,
Every step, a new embrace.

Through the valleys, over peaks,
With the dawn, the soul it seeks,
Ephemeral journeys, days and weeks,
Wisdom found in nature's tweaks.

Starlit paths and morning dew,
Guiding us to places new,
Ephemeral journeys, visions true,
In each moment, life anew.

Wanderlust within our hearts,
Turning where the journey starts,
Ephemeral journeys, sacred arts,
Etched in time, as it departs.

Grainy Chronicles

Grain by grain, the stories told,
In the chronicles of old,
Every grain, a secret hold,
Woven threads of life unfold.

Through the sands, tales of yore,
Waves of time on history's shore,
Grainy chronicles explore,
Echoes of what came before.

Pages turned in silt and dust,
Legends kept in ancient trust,
Grainy chronicles, we must,
Listen close and read just.

Desert winds, they softly sigh,
Songs of time as they pass by,
Grainy chronicles, ally,
To the dreams we hold up high.

Past and present intertwined,
Grainy chronicles remind,
In their depths, truths we find,
Stories etched within our mind.

Ocean's Diary

In the embrace of tides, I pen my tale,
With foam as ink, on waves that flail.
Days are chapters, nights are notes,
In this grand diary, my heart floats.

Sunrise paints the margins red,
Moonlight writes the dreams we've shed.
Fishes flit with news untold,
Shells and sands, secrets unfold.

Currents whisper in ancient tongue,
Songs of sailors forever young.
Pages turn with each great swell,
Where stories of the ocean dwell.

On tempest winds, my thoughts set sail,
Finding love in every gale.
Storms may tear the lines apart,
Yet always mends the ocean's heart.

A diary vast, with boundless pages,
Preludes to the future, echoes of ages.
In myriad tongues, its verses sing,
For in its depths, life eternally springs.

Wave-Kissed Paths

Where sea meets land, my feet do tread,
On paths where ancient waters spread.
Each step a mark, a fleeting trace,
Yet waves come forth to fill the space.

Sea spray whispers tales of yore,
Of lovers lost and found once more.
Pebbles gleam with laughter past,
In the dance of waves, shadows are cast.

Footprints on this sand expire,
Yet leave behind a soft desire.
To walk again where waves caress,
To feel the ocean's fond impress.

Each tide, a painter, ever grand,
Reshapes the paths on shifting sand.
A canvas, fresh with morning dew,
Of infinite journeys, old and anew.

In wave-kissed paths, my heart does weave,
A tale of moments we shall never grieve.
For in each step and wave's caress,
I find the boundless sea's address.

Whispered Trails

Through forest shades and moonlit nights,
Whispered trails lead hidden flights.
Leaves speak secrets, winds confide,
In nature's realm, our fears subside.

Each step reveals a silent song,
Of roots entwined, of paths so long.
Branches bow with ancient lore,
Their stories told from core to core.

Stars above our guideposts true,
Lighting paths we never knew.
In chorus with the breeze, we find,
The trails where spirits are enshrined.

In whispered words, the wilds speak,
Of strength in silence, power in meek.
Guided by these unseen hands,
We tread through life's enchanted lands.

Each footfall on this hallowed ground,
Leaves a mark that's soft yet sound.
Whispered trails of life's grand quest,
Lead our hearts to endless rest.

Impermanent Footprints

Along the shore, I leave my mark,
In dance with waves, from light to dark.
Footprints fade with every tide,
Yet something deeper does abide.

Each step a moment, brief yet bright,
Imprinted on the sands of light.
Tides may wash these prints away,
But memories in heart shall stay.

Waves erase, yet don't dispel,
The stories that these prints do tell.
Of joys, of tears, and wanderings,
Of fleeting, cherished human things.

Though footprints may not last for long,
Their essence etches life's sweet song.
In transient steps, our souls take flight,
To realms of day and realms of night.

Impermanent, yet ever true,
Footprints write a tale anew.
On shores of time, where waves persist,
In every step, life's bold insist.

Ephemeral Marks

In sand, we carve our fleeting names,
Each wave that crashes, shifts our claims.
A moment held in time's soft hands,
Only to be washed from lands.

Footsteps fading, stories blend,
To nature's will, we must attend.
Transient as the morning dew,
Marks erased, life's page anew.

Moonlit whispers on the shore,
Remind us what marks were before.
Ever-changing, never still,
We trace our paths upon life's hill.

Silent messages we send,
In transient forms, they wend.
In sand and stone, we leave our trace,
Only to vanish, without a place.

Cycles of the endless sea,
Teach us about ephemerality.
Marks we leave, like summer's rain,
Are washed away, without disdain.

Coastal Echoes

Whispers on the coastal breeze,
Carry tales of distant seas.
Surf and sand in harmony,
Sing of lasting symphony.

Gulls call out their ancient cries,
Underneath the boundless skies.
Waves embrace the steadfast shore,
Echoing forevermore.

Shells and driftwood, tokens found,
Stories in their silence bound.
Tides that ebb and tides that flow,
Shape the world that we all know.

Sailboats on the horizon's line,
Journey to where the stars align.
Harbors filled with sights and scenes,
Of sailors' whispered dreams.

In the twilight, colors blend,
Sun and sea become a friend.
Where earth and ocean gently meet,
Life's echoes softly, sweetly beat.

Journey Across Grains

In the desert's golden sea,
A journey waits for you and me.
Dunes embrace the endless sky,
Underneath the sun's watchful eye.

Camels stride with steady grace,
Tracks we leave, the sands erase.
Whispers of the ancient past,
Carried on the warm wind's blast.

Oases gleam like jewels bright,
Mirage turns day to dreamlike night.
Across the grains, we find our way,
Through arid lands where shadows play.

Stars above in vast expanse,
Guide us with their ageless dance.
Footsteps trace a fleeting line,
Intertwined with space and time.

Nomads of this barren ground,
Hear the quiet, profound sound.
In the still of night we find,
The journey's spirit, unconfined.

Transient Trails

Paths we tread, so briefly known,
Winding through the great unknown.
Silent steps on wooded trails,
Where every whisper softly hails.

Dappled light through leaves that sway,
Guides our footsteps on the way.
Crickets serenade the dusk,
In a world so fresh and husk.

Mountains rise and valleys fall,
Nature's wonders, we recall.
Transient moments, fleeting gleam,
Life's an ever-flowing stream.

Raindrops kiss the forest floor,
Transitory as before.
Frozen still in memory's chase,
Yet vanish without a trace.

Trails we carve through fleeting time,
Ephemeral, pure, and sublime.
Transient as the twilight's hue,
We find our paths anew, anew.

Ghosts of the Tide

Whispers ride on the midnight air
Specters dance with lunar light
Salt and wind, a phantom pair
Haunting shores throughout the night

Echoes of laughter, long since gone
Footsteps lost in shifting sand
Ethereal voices greet the dawn
Ghosts of the tide, hand in hand

Moonlit ripples lull the soul
Waves give life to memories
To the past, they pay their toll
Unseen echoes across the seas

In the silence, hear their cries
Countless dreams, now adrift
In the waves, the history lies
In their folds, all spirits lift

Vestiges of Waves

Fleeting moments, ocean's song
Whispers of where we once stood
Stories told, both short and long
Carved in currents, understood

Sunlight glints on ancient scars
Ridges formed by time and tide
Life and love in sand and stars
Ephemeral, where secrets hide

Moon pulls seas in gentle dance
Tidal rhythms, age-old flow
Vestiges of chance romance
Sway where only mysteries know

From vast depths to beach's reach
Waves leave traces, paths they pave
In their crash, the lessons teach
Life's within the vestiges of waves

Crumbling Paths

Steps once firm now fade away
Footfalls lost in broken stone
Memories within clay
Echoing where dreams are sown

Time wears down what once was proud
Diminishing each proud crest
Dust replaced the cheering crowd
Crumbling paths now laid to rest

Beneath the foliage, stories deep
Whispers of what used to be
Histories in shadows keep
Silent truths for eyes to see

Nature claims its gentle due
Overgrowth where roads unfold
Paths dissolve in earthy hue
Into fragments, bright and old

Whispered Coastline

Waves lap softly, murmured tales
Zephyrs weave through coastal dreams
Whispers rise as sunlight pales
In the twilight, magic gleams

Shells and pebbles, secrets keep
In their silence, voices call
Whispered coastline, currents sweep
Mysteries ensnare us all

Even starry nights hold tight
Echoes from the sea's embrace
In their glow, the past alight
Stories swirl in foamy lace

Nature's breath upon the shore
Each wave is a gentle brush
Whispered coastline speaks once more
In their sound, a timeless hush

Hushed Tidewalk

Soft whispers grace the moonlit shore,
A dance of waves, a gentle lore.
Footprints fade in silken sand,
Echoes linger, hand in hand.

The world is still, a breathless hush,
Stars above in wild rush.
Midnight's secrets softly speak,
In the night, the solace seek.

Cool breeze weaves through whispering trees,
Soul at peace, time seems to freeze.
Quietude of night's embrace,
A tender smile in shadows trace.

Mysteries of the deep arise,
In night's embrace, no disguise.
The tidewalk weaves a silent tune,
Underneath the silver moon.

Heartbeats sync with ebb and flow,
In this space, the magic show.
Hushed tidewalk, where dreams ignite,
Underneath the cloak of night.

Nature's Diary

Pages turned by the morning light,
A symphony from dawn to night.
Whispers of the forest green,
In Nature's diary, scenes unseen.

Meadows hum with bees and breeze,
Leaves converse in rustling tease.
Rivers write in fluid prose,
Flowing tales where beauty grows.

Mountains stand with wisdom old,
Stories in their ridges told.
Sky's canvas, colors bright,
Dancing with the birds in flight.

Every dawn, a fresh new page,
Sunrise casts a golden stage.
Gentle rain in rhythmic patter,
Inscribe joys in Nature's matter.

Flower petals soft as ink,
Secret thoughts in morning's wink.
Nature's diary, day and night,
Chronicling the world's delight.

Beneath the Waves

Secrets hold in watery graves,
Mysteries hush beneath the waves.
Whales sing songs of yesteryears,
Echoes caught in ocean's tears.

Coral realms, a vibrant lore,
Guardians of the ocean floor.
Schools of silver dart and gleam,
In the current's gentle dream.

Shadows play in azure deep,
Where the ancient secrets sleep.
Whispers through the kelp forest,
Guardians of oceans' rest.

Mariners of old once sailed,
Now in legends, fish's tale.
Sunlight weaves through turquoise veils,
Guiding dreams in ocean trails.

Depths where time and stories blend,
In the sea's enfolding bend.
Beneath the waves, the heart of blue,
A world unseen yet always true.

Coastline's Memory

Contours traced by time and sea,
The coastline's memory, wild and free.
Stories carved in craggy rocks,
Echoes of the seabird flocks.

Golden sands in moonlit glow,
Recollect the tides of long ago.
Footsteps washed yet left behind,
In the heart, the soul's inclined.

Waves in rhythmic, ceaseless call,
Recall the shipwrecks, rise and fall.
Coves where whispers never cease,
In the sea's eternal peace.

Each grain of sand, a story keeps,
Of silent dawns, where secrets sleeps.
Breezes tell of journeys past,
Of love and loss, the joy that lasts.

Memories etched in coastal line,
Markers of the passing time.
In each curve, a tale to see,
In coastline's ancient memory.

Ephemeral Prints

In the morning dew, our traces thin,
Steps fade, where walks begin.
Whispers of time, footprints blend,
Shadows dance, and swiftly end.

Clouds of thought, a fleeting show,
Imprints lost, in flow they go.
Moments pass, like sand through sieve,
Our marks ephemeral, ineffusive.

Leaves will fall and winds will churn,
Paths erased with every turn.
Memory holds what ground forsakes,
Through days, and nights, our journey makes.

Echoes of the past will bloom,
In fleeting silence, room to room.
In every heart, a soft imprint,
Of love or sorrow, briefly stint.

Come the dawn, we walk anew,
Steps like whispers, soft and true.
Ephemeral prints in morning's glance,
Gone with time, a silent dance.

Ripples of Recall

Still waters hold a quiet tale,
Of whispered winds, and strangers pale.
Ripples dance on memory's face,
Revealing moments, time's embrace.

The silent pond, a still memoir,
Reflects the wishes cast afar.
In ripples deep, the secrets flow,
Of yesteryears, and hearts aglow.

Each wave, a story, old and new,
Captured in the morning dew.
The breeze will stir, and yet remain,
The ripples of recall, unclaimed.

The moon will rise, reflections gleam,
On waters dark, a muted dream.
Beneath the tranquil, surface bright,
Lie echoes of the silent night.

Recall the ripples, soft and true,
Each one a whisper, of what's due.
In stillness, life begins to call,
Through ripples of recall, we fall.

Steps of Solitude

On quiet paths, alone I tread,
Where silence reigns, and thoughts are spread.
Each step a whisper in the air,
In solitude, I find my care.

Beneath the trees, the shadows play,
Guiding me with light's soft ray.
The rustling leaves, a gentle song,
In steps of solitude, I belong.

The world outside, a distant hum,
In solitude, my heart is drum.
The rhythm beats within my chest,
In steps of solitude, I rest.

On mountain paths, by streams so clear,
Solitude's embrace is near.
With every step, I find anew,
A world serene, just me and you.

In solitude, I walk the line,
Between the world and what's divine.
Each step a journey, deep and wide,
In steps of solitude, I glide.

Waves and Wanderings

Oceans vast, with waves that call,
To distant shores where dreams befall.
In wanderings, we find our way,
Through tide and tempest, night and day.

The currents pull, the winds do guide,
Across the sea's expanse so wide.
With every crest, a story told,
Of ancient mariners, brave and bold.

In wanderings, the heart does yearn,
For places new, a world to learn.
Waves do crash and gently kiss,
The sands of time, in fleeting bliss.

Beneath the stars, the ocean's breath,
Whispers tales of life and death.
In wanderings, we come to see,
The waves are mirrors to the sea.

With every wave, and wandering so,
We chart the course where spirits go.
Through ebb and flow, we find our being,
In waves and wanderings, all-seeing.